KAZUO SHINOHARA : THE UMBRELLA HOUSE PROJECT

Edited by
Christian Dehli, Andrea Grolimund

Vitra
Design
Museum

INTRODUCTION

Some three years ago, visiting Tokyo, we learned that Umbrella House (1961)—one of the smallest of the iconic early timber-framed houses designed by the Japanese architect Kazuo Shinohara (1925–2006)—was in danger of demolition. We had been unable to visit the house itself, but after we returned to Switzerland, Heritage Houses Trust, a Japanese non-profit organization specialized in finding new owners for endangered, historically important houses in Japan, asked our architectural practice for help. HHT were hoping to find a new owner for Umbrella House, who could somehow preserve and guarantee its existence in the long term.

In the summer of 2019, Rolf Fehlbaum from Vitra also visited Japan and met the two architects Kazuo Sejima and Ryue Nishizawa from the well-known architectural firm SANAA in Tokyo, which had close prior connections to Vitra. Over dinner, they spoke of a house by Kazuo Shinohara that was likely soon to be destroyed. Fehlbaum was irritated that an architectural masterpiece could simply be torn down like that. A few weeks later, talks had progressed and Fehlbaum was asked if he would like to acquire Umbrella House and relocate it to the Vitra Campus in Weil am Rhein, Germany.

Without hesitation, Fehlbaum agreed to save it if no other owner could be found. This stroke of good fortune effectively saved Umbrella House and Rolf Fehlbaum contacted us in November 2020, asking if we would be interested in helping to reconstruct Shinohara's masterpiece on their campus. This publication tells the story of Umbrella House from its initial construction in Tokyo in 1961 to its preservation a little more than sixty years later in Weil am Rhein.

Christian Dehli, Andrea Grolimund

UMBRELLA HOUSE
AND
THE STRUGGLES
OF
KAZUO SHINOHARA

:

Ryue Nishizawa

I first visited Umbrella House in the spring of 2020, when the work of dismantling the house was beginning in preparation for its move to the Vitra Campus. The house was much smaller than I had imagined. In that respect it typified the scale and layout of the average Japanese house of its time, built as it was in the early 1960s, when the scent of the postwar recovery period still lingered. But it was anything but an ordinary house. For one thing, it had a square plan topped by a parasol-like pyramidal roof. If the most economical, and common, design for conventional wood-framed Japanese houses of the day was a rectangular plan with a gabled roof, then the design of this small residence made it an outlier. Most Japanese architects, upon seeing this juxtaposition of square plan and pyramidal roof, would probably recognize that Kazuo Shinohara was attempting to build a modest, ordinary home in the image of the Jōdo-dō (Pure Land Hall) at Jōdo-ji temple in Hyogo prefecture.

Other inspirations for Umbrella House besides the Jōdo-dō at Jōdo-ji also come to mind. One is the traditional Japanese farmhouse, or *minka*. The dining area that occupies the south side of Umbrella House is floored with wood, but the space itself is equivalent to the earthen-floored *doma* kitchen area found in a standard *minka*. Indeed, the house appears to be based on several types of classical Japanese architecture—and yet it is indubitably a work of contemporary architecture. The arrangement of the spaces, the combinations of various elements—these aspects can be described as contemporary. As I explored every nook and cranny of this little house, inside and out, the thought "I want to try this" simply occurred to me. What I wanted to try was to build the house myself from the original plans. Being the sort of architect who always wants to try something new, I find it hard to explain why I would be seized with the desire to replicate an existing work of architecture. The closest analogy I can think of is a musician who reads the score or hears a performance of a past work and feels an urge to perform that piece himself. Somewhere in that house, I sensed a universal quality that I wanted to experience for myself. Furthermore, I sensed something contemporary in Shinohara's effort to achieve that quality.

Umbrella House contains several major architectural languages that give life to the house. Take, for example, the oversized eaves, which evoke shrine and temple architecture; the square plan; the presence of both *doma* and tatami-floored spaces; the 3:4 proportional division of the square; the main entry situated right on the east-west center line, in direct contravention of the 3:4 division; the framework supporting the pyramidal roof; the kitchen protruding from the square plan; and the slender freestanding pillar at one corner of the tatami room. I believe I am not alone in seeing the Jōdo-dō and the *minka* as the primary sources of these various languages. When one attempts to apply architectural language that one has previously admired to one's own practice, however, various struggles ensue over such issues as: what elevation ratio to establish between the square and pyramidal sections; how to divide the living space in two while retaining the sensation of spatial unity under one large roof; where to place the entrance and the bath; how to maintain horizontal rigidity while exposing the interior to the roof frame. The process of applying these ideas to an actual house is, in practice, one of trial and error. Shinohara himself struggled to resolve these issues, and was not entirely successful. If anything, the architecture of the house embodies both successes and failures. The point I want to make here is not that Shinohara was or wasn't victorious in the struggles he faced to build this house, but that the struggles themselves are fascinating, and extremely typical of Shinohara. They include numerous experiments and contrivances that suggest—contrary to the frequent image of Shinohara the austere perfectionist—a man full of ideas who was imaginative and open-minded in his creation of space. The struggles we see here are, without exception, full of vitality. They also feel very contemporary—alive today, not just some relic from the past.

The Swiss pianist and conductor Edwin Fischer once said that playing Beethoven's piano sonatas entailed negotiating between two perilous paths. The first such path was that of "self-expression"—the performer's use of Beethoven's score to express himself. The second danger lay in pursuing a blind obedience to the score that would produce a mechanical replication of the piece. Anyone attempting to play these sonatas, Fischer averred, was bound to confront the challenge of forging a middle path between these two hazards. I believe his words apply not only to people confronting the piano sonatas of Beethoven, but to practitioners of other artistic endeavors as well. They are particularly relevant to those of us engaged in the work of architectural design. Consider that all, or nearly all, the ingredients an architect brings to the design of a building—structures, building methods, theories, floors, walls, roofs, windows, pillars, beams, materials—are things of the past. The architect uses these ingredients of the past to create the future. Fischer also said that there is only one way to hew to the middle path, and that is truly to love Beethoven's sonatas.

I recalled Fischer's words more than once during my visit to Umbrella House. When Shinohara built it, surely he was visualizing the Jōdo-dō of Jōdo-ji, or any number of traditional *minka*, when he said to himself, "I want to try this." He faced the struggle of building this house with the desire that is imperative for anyone who intends to create the future from the past. Regardless of whether he succeeded or failed, Shinohara wanted to walk the middle path of which Fischer spoke—neither the path of rote reproduction of the Jōdo-dō, nor that of self-expression for its own sake. I don't know if Shinohara suffered in the course of his struggles, or if he enjoyed them. Most likely both. I suspect they were, in fact, pleasurable—at the least, he must have felt they were worth the trouble. Shinohara's fundamental struggle, with the question of how to give form to the many architectural encounters that had transformed him in the past, was unlikely to be resolved in this one small structure, as became clear in the course of building it. The struggle carried over to his next project, and the next, and the next. Architects who are familiar with Shinohara will recognize from a single visit to Umbrella House that it is preceded by a number of classical Japanese structures, and moreover, that Shinohara's struggle with this house presaged the birth of his House in White (1966). In my view, the significance of Umbrella House is clear from its position at the very center of that continuum.

Looking north toward artificially elevated building plot
in Nerima Ward, Tokyo, 1959

Looking south f

uilt terraced site, 1959

South and west elevations of 1:50 scale model, 1959/1960

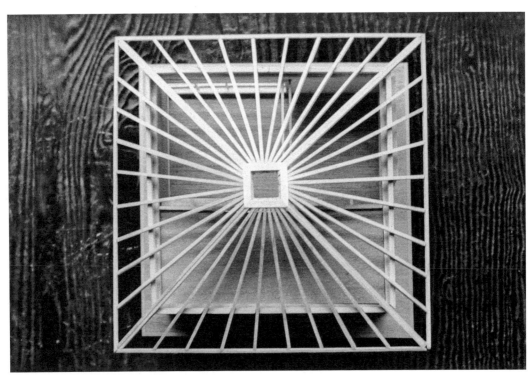

Roof structure of 1:50 scale model showing position of timber fan-rafters
joined at top steel base plate, 1959/1960

South façade under construction, view from be

ining wall before start of roof framework, 1960

Roof structure viewed from future south façade
wall aperture, 1960

Roof under construction with fan-rafters in place and held
together at top by open steel base plate, 1960

View from northwest with comple

structure in place, 1960

West flank of roof being decked, 1961

UMBRELLA HOUSE

:

Kazuo Shinohara

My essay, "A House Is Art," was written in early 1962, the same year as the design of this Umbrella House. The essay was one of my frontal attacks on the situation of house designing at the time. Now that rationalism and functionalism, the main forces of the time, had collapsed, architecture and design, let alone housing, had become artistic, even if not exactly in the sense of the word I meant at the time. I need not repeat here the same argument. In 1967 I also wrote on this subject in "Houses Have Already Become Art."

This house is the smallest house I have ever designed. While I was designing it, I was also working on The House at Chigasaki, one of the largest houses I have ever designed. In the process, I began to conceive the idea of 'wasteful space' as a basic idea. In such a small house, however, it was impossible to develop 'wasteful space' as a major theme. I thought, though, that the expression of 'wasteful space' in a small house would be possible through making immanent the void space or void space with its insufficiency.

To put it more directly, I thought, the expression of 'wasteful space' in a small house would be possible through the extreme simplification of the dwelling functions.

To build this small house, I commuted to the building site in the suburbs of Tokyo on many days. On cold winter days the road to the building site seemed to be very long. I wondered about the rationale for designing, supervising its construction, and completing such a small house in the midst of this large industrialized society. Not the social production of housing but the creation of space which strongly appeals to people defines the work of house design. Unless they become art, houses have no reason for being. My conviction that houses are art was born out of my struggle with this small house. I wished to express the force of space contained in the *doma* (earthen-floor room) of an old Japanese farmhouse by means of the geometric design of a *karakasa* (paper umbrella).

PLANS
:
1:100

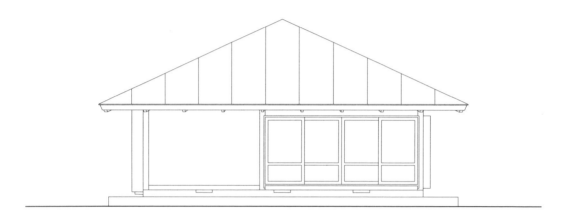

South elevation

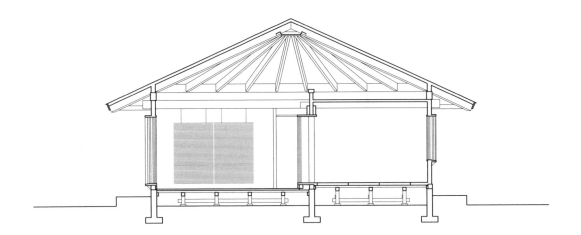

Section

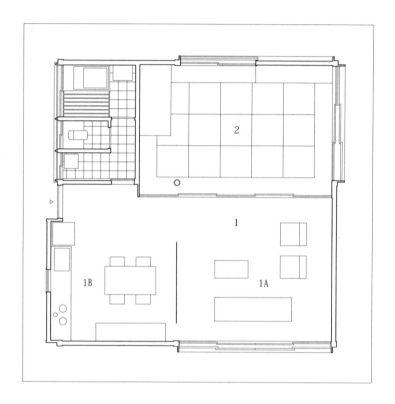

First floor plan

1 – Main room (1A – Living room, 1B – Dining room/kitchen)
2 – Tatami room

Ceiling plan

CONSTRUCTION
AND
RECONSTRUCTION
:

Christian Dehli
Andrea Grolimund

2019/02/20 Umbrella House in Nerima Ward, Tokyo

2019/02/20 Living room viewed from loft

2019/12/23 Living room and
adjacent tatami room

2020/06/26 Carefully removing original furniture

2020/06/18 Labeling original flooring before transport to warehouse in Japan

2020/07/13 Dismantling of second floor

2020/07/10 Cladding removed from interior walls before disassembly

2020/07/10 View into dismantled tatami room

2020/08/07 Removal of fan-rafters

2020/09/03 Dismantled structural elements at Fuhki Construction's warehouse
in Chiba prefecture, outside Tokyo

2020/09/03 Measuring polished Japanese cypress post

2020/09/03   Discussion on how to restore and adjust fan-rafters

2021/09/12 Various oil stain color tests on different
types of wood

2020/09/12 Reviewing working drawings and list of
structural elements

2021/04/16 Ensemble of new and restored timber elements

2021/04/16 Construction materials being loaded before
transfer to shipper

2021/04/26 Disassembled elements packed in
plywood storage units by Nippon Express

2021/04/26 Preparing boxes for loading into shipping containers

2021/04/26 Entire Umbrella House fitted and
packed into two shipping containers

One of Kazuo Shinohara's acknowledged masterpieces, Umbrella House, was designed and erected in 1961 in the then exurbs of Tokyo by the young, mathematically grounded Japanese architect (1925–2006) who is universally well-known today. In 2022 the house found a new home in Europe on the Vitra Campus in Weil am Rhein, southwestern Germany near Basel.

Umbrella House is one of the few remaining houses from Shinohara's so-called First Style. This dwelling is of great architectural-historical interest, and its composition and detailing between modernism and tradition still amazes those with the good fortune to have seen it. The 55 m² wooden house with a nearly square footprint of 7.50×7.50 m was secured from demolition by Rolf Fehlbaum, Chairman Emeritus of Vitra. Owing to its massive timber-framed construction with non-load-bearing infill walls, it was possible with some effort to relocate the house. It was scheduled to be transported shortly after our first meeting and visit to the future construction site in December 2020. Shipping an entire house from Japan to Germany was a fantastic undertaking for us. Newly prefabricated house elements loaded onto trucks have become a familiar sight, but disassembling an entire preexisting house and sending it on a long sea journey was completely new to our architectural experience.

Umbrella House originally stood in Hayamiya, Nerima Ward, Tokyo Metropolis. This district was originally rural, but in the postwar period it gradually morphed into a denser residential neighborhood. The client for the house was Shozo Kawai, an employee of the Japanese telecom company Kokusai Denshin Denwa (KDD, now KDDI), who occupied it after completion together with his wife and young daughter (as well as the live-in domestic that was still common at the time). In fact the house was only built thanks to a Japanese government loan, which was unusual in the immediate postwar years.

After her parents died, the daughter Emi Kawai inherited Umbrella House. Due to inheritance tax and the densely populated neighborhood, Ms Kawai decided to move. It was also known that a major road construction project would have affected her property, forcing the house to be demolished sooner or later. Umbrella House went up for sale most likely as a teardown, since older houses are seen in Japan as of little value and there is scarcely any interest in maintenance concerns. Usually, a Japanese home is built economically and meant to last for one or two generations at most.

These considerations were why the non-profit Heritage Houses Trust sought a buyer to save the architecturally valuable house from demolition. It soon became clear that Umbrella House was unlikely to remain in Japan. Land prices in Japan, especially in Tokyo, are astronomical and while older vernacular houses are frequently disassembled and moved to new locations, a house of this era had little appeal. Since most of Shinohara's earlier houses create their own internal world and emanate from an "idea" rather than drawing inspiration from their surroundings, First and Second Style works could theoretically be relocated anywhere in the world, construction methods permitting, without undermining the quality of their architectural statement.

Due to the COVID-19 pandemic, a massive container shortage occurred in Asia in early 2021 as a result of inactivity in US ports, where backups multiplied. For a brief while, prices increased by a factor of ten. The scheduled date for shipping Umbrella House was therefore postponed again and again until containers finally became available in May 2021. The dismantled house arrived in Weil am Rhein within two months. The huge wooden packing cases were unloaded from their containers with forklifts and carefully unpacked under the watchful supervision of Vitra's own project manager Christian Germadnik and ourselves. We felt as if we were part of Buster Keaton's silent comedy *One Week*, released in September 1920. All components were neatly packed and labeled in Japanese. First, the hundreds of parts were sorted, laid out and verified in an otherwise empty warehouse near the Vitra Campus.

Umbrella House had been meticulously documented, measured, and disassembled in

Tokyo before its journey. Any broken or missing parts of the wooden structure were made good by Fuhki Construction at their specialized workshop using the appropriate wood: Japanese cypress, Japanese cedar, or Oregon pine. Over the years, Umbrella House had undergone modifications to meet the changing needs of the Kawai family. Extra service spaces were added on the north, the main entry repositioned, bath and toilet facilities reorganized, and the kitchen modernized and enlarged. Importantly, the roof had been extended and resurfaced. These adjustments did not involve Shinohara and so did not address the architectural qualities of the original design. Therefore, our aim was to rebuild Shinohara's Umbrella House as intended in his 1960 working drawings, including the previously unrealized, originally designated rubble retaining wall fronting the site. Certain elements have been repainted several times over the years, while other finishes had exceeded their useful life and required replacement.

In the spring of 2021, a building site was designated on the Vitra Campus. Umbrella House, never intended as a pavilion situated on an open field, was slightly raised to contrast with the surrounding furniture-production facilities; as well as two further architectural icons, a Petrol Station by Jean Prouvé (1953), and a small Dome (1954/1975) by Richard Buckminster Fuller. Meanwhile, the ancient Jōdo-dō at Jōdo-ji, Ono, Hyogo prefecture, discussed above as providing a historical reference for the original design of the house, is also subtly recalled by the new more open setting. A hedge ensures the privacy that is of such importance to the Japanese home. Also, the cardinal points of the site needed to correspond to those of the original location, this being the only way to retain the desired natural lighting situation inside the house.

The architect Masaru Otsuka and his team from Tokyo Tech participated in the entire reconstruction process via email, repeated online meetings, and the on-site installation of a webcam. New execution drawings were created by the Yamazaki and Okuyama labs at Tokyo Tech. Our team headed by Prof. Shin-ichi Okuyama was faced with constant challenges. For example, it was our intention to keep the Japanese electrical switches and sockets in their original positions. The problem was that the 110-V electrical system operating in Japan does not match the 230-V capacity most frequently found in Europe. Nonetheless, the switches were rendered functional and German sockets installed beneath the Japanese socket covers. As practicing architects, we often had to explain Japanese details unfamiliar to German craftspeople carrying out the work. Yet in the end, local subcontractors were proud of what they had achieved and were even able to adopt some of the Japanese work for use in other projects. Regarding the timber fittings, numerous details are solved differently in Japan and Germany, and with varying standards. The new reinforced concrete foundation work had to meet requirements of the German-cum-EU standard known as DIN. The frame surmounting it was the restored Japanese 1960s original, with new surfaces applied inside and out.

The original blue and yellow silk wallpapers in the tatami room could be ordered and custom-replicated by one of the last silk wallpaper manufacturers in Kyoto, restoring the room to its subtle colorfulness. Unfortunately, all traces of the original wall covering had disappeared over time. We mainly knew the house from black and white photographs, so it was exciting to have color suddenly restored to the interior for the first time in over half a century, both in the tatami room and in the living-room areas. For example, the living room furniture, designed by Shinohara in collaboration with Katsuhiko Shiraishi and upholstered in an irregular nubbed fabric of cerulean blue linen competes with a deep lilac carpet. Basically, all furniture pieces were designed by the architect, since the quality of mass-produced postwar furniture was so poor that Shinohara had little choice but to take on this extra role. The two blinds of unsplit bamboo (sudare) were also selected by the architect. Over the years, various pieces of furniture had disappeared. To show the house in full continuity and scale, it was important to restore existing furniture or reconstruct what was missing. It was fortunate that we had the support of Vitra, an experienced partner in furniture-making. Since no working drawings for the furniture are extant, designs had to be reconstructed based on photos of similar furniture that Shinohara had designed for other houses at that time. The missing kitchen installation was cleverly (albeit non-functionally) replicated for this house.

Kazuo Shinohara found it satisfying to work with pictorial artists during the first of his dedicated Four Styles. On the house's sliding doors (fusuma), which separate the tatami room from the living room, there are five paintings on gold leaf by the almost contemporary artist and set designer Setsu Asakura (1922–2014). Fortunately, these were still present alongside the various layers of newsprint patching on the fusuma. These delicate works of art could be carefully removed and glued back on after the fusuma had been re-covered with new Japanese washi paper. Another painted work by the same artist hangs in the living room.

Restored woodwork, refurbished and newly constructed furniture, freshly painted walls and ceiling panels, new shoji screens, and deep-cleaned and polished wooden flooring now present the house in its original appearance and allow the visitor to enter this unique architectural masterpiece from 1960s Japan. The traces of time are still visible in the elaborately restored house, with all its scratches and stories, which now shines in renewed splendor. This is also aided by the new square tatami mats, carefully selected floor tiles, and thoroughly restored fusuma.

Thus, it should be stressed that Umbrella House is no "ordinary" Japanese home, but rather a precise design comprising spatially new experiences. The lofty symmetrical under-roof space, conferred by its metaphorical umbrella, was completely unknown to conventional residential building and gave the house its name, Umbrella House *(Karakasa no ie)*. The visible rafters are reminiscent of a large traditional Japanese umbrella, which consists of a bamboo structure covered in oiled, hence waterproof, paper and used particularly during the Edo period.

After arriving in Weil am Rhein, all original structural woodwork, as well as the wooden cladding of the living room walls, was laboriously freed of the many different layers of oil paint and varnish applied over the years. This work was crucial for the overall appearance and lasted several weeks. Only then was the timber frame erected and the house reconstructed. Numerous color tests followed in conjunction with our online meetings with

Tokyo. The various wooden elements—such as the supporting structure, wall cladding, floor, ladder, and window frames—exhibit different luminosity and sheens, which we knew from the contrasts portrayed in existing black-and-white photographs.

It is hardly surprising that the exterior cladding of the house had suffered over the decades and needed almost complete replacing. It is made of white-painted cement board and, in the kitchen area, diagonally applied Japanese cypress-wood sheathing. Although once replaced with asphalt shingles of a common type, the original roof was made of a new and experimental material branded "Superalloy", a sheet metal in combination with rubber or gum. This had begun to leak, so that the rafters near the roof ridge were starting to rot. One probable reason for this is that the owners equipped the typically unheated house with oil-burning space heaters, causing condensation at the apex of the roof. It is also unclear why in 1961 the roof was equipped with a peripheral rain gutter, which in no way corresponds to Shinohara's original working drawings and would even seem to contradict the metaphor of the umbrella. Our new roofing of broad, untreated aluminum sheets comes closest to the original roof. The material supports the initial notion of a roof that is as smooth, geometrically precise, and sharply profiled as possible.

As previously mentioned, an addition was made in the former bathroom and toilet area, which thus no longer conformed to Shinohara's original scheme. As part of the reconstruction program, we decided with Tokyo Tech and Vitra to reinstall a simple toilet in this area. There is a small adjacent kitchenette. During the entire reconstruction, we took into account how the house could be used easily by small numbers of interested people, as well as casual visitors.

From Tokyo Tech colleagues and friends, we know that Kazuo Shinohara would have been pleased that Umbrella House was saved from demolition. The fact that the house now stands on the European continent would not bother him in the least; indeed it would have been the source of pleasure and pride. Throughout his last actively creative years, that is to say during his Fourth Style, Shinohara continually participated in competitions across Europe, but without success. Now instead, we pay him the honor of preserving one of his masterpieces. It is unique that a private residence from Kazuo Shinohara's First Style can now be visited by appointed request and will receive the attention and scrutiny that the masterpiece deserves.

2021/06/21 Shipping containers having arrived at
Weil am Rhein, Germany, opened by local staff

2021/06/21 Moving storage units from one of the shipping containers
for eventual reassembly at Vitra Campus

2021/07/05 Opening the plywood storage unit
containing the top steel base plate

2021/07/05 Vetting of all shipped elements after
arrival in Germany

2021/07/30 Removal of older layers of oil stain, paint, and lacquer,
applied over the years on timber frame

2021/07/30 Initial joining trials of timber frame

2021/07/30 Verification of site orientation
at Vitra Campus

2021/10/06 Timber framing erected on new
reinforced concrete foundation

2021/10/07 Beginning of roof assembly process

2021/10/07 First fan-rafters being joined
to corner of top steel base plate

2021/10/19 Purlins being mounted on completed
roof structure

2022/03/08 Completion of new roofing made of
broad untreated aluminium sheets

2022/03/08 Adjustment of minor elements before
painting the interior

2022/04/06 Preparation for interior paintwork

2022/05/27 Installation of kitchen units

2022/05/30 Restored fusuma installed
between living and tatami rooms

2022/05/30 Preparation for planting before
starting exterior paintwork

AN ARCHITECT'S DNA
REVEALED
IN A SINGLE WORK

:

Shin-ichi Okuyama
David B. Stewart

Having arrived at the recently restored Jōdo-dō, where a vivid contrast between its vermilion columns and beams and white freshly plastered wall left us somehow ill at ease—and, in addition, the external appearance of its unusual pyramidal roof struck one as awkward—we felt a bit disappointed after the long journey to the Jōdo-ji temple in West Japan. Yet, once I followed the chief priest inside, I found myself in a magnificent space.

There, unexpectedly, I met with the vast space of an invisible power, such as I [could scarcely believe to be part of] our history. It proved a compelling space, whose simplicity I was tempted to compare with the [European] Romanesque and its structural boldness with the Gothic.

Kazuo Shinohara, *Jūtaku-kenchiku*, 1964, pp. 61–62 [trans.]*

* Except when sourced from a publication named in English, all translations are jointly by the authors of the present article.

INTRODUCTION:
THE JŌDO-DŌ AT JŌDO-JI

This account is from the architect Kazuo Shinohara's first published book and refers to Jōdo-dō (1197), which is the main Pure Land Hall of Jōdo-ji at Ono (Hyogo prefecture, west of Osaka). The Hall was erected by the venerable monk Chōgen (1121–1206), who had made three separate journeys to Song-dynasty China toward the end of the twelfth century (1167–76). This Pure Land Hall is said to be one of the few ancient buildings in Japan that preserves an original Buddhist architectural prototype (the admittedly rare so-called Big Buddha style). It manifests in our own time a unique Chinese style of nearly a millennium ago.

The Pure Land Hall at Ono is a simple square in plan with twelve pillars set at intervals of six meters defining its perimeter. At the center, four taller pillars are inserted into the grid to support the upper region of its roof. A bay is thereby created surrounding the 5.3-meter-high iconic Amitabha triad statue of the Buddha of the Western Paradise flanked by two sacred attendants. A multitude of subsidiary beams and structural

Jōdo-dō, Jōdo-ji, Ono, Hyogo Prefecture, 1194

framing elements penetrate these four tall central columns, creating an extraordinarily unified structural system upholding the unusual 18-meter square pyramidal roof of the hall. Since no false ceiling intervenes, all these structural members can be seen from below, as well as the barely perceptible concave curvature *(sori)* of the roof, which is relatively unusual in later Buddhist temples.

In fair weather the setting sun penetrates the western wall of the hall's lattice-shuttered façade, reverberating off the floor of Japanese cypress and illuminating the complex ensemble of vermilion-painted rafters. For a short time, the entire space appears aflame from behind the great triad of Buddhist statues. This fantastical scene was perceived by the faithful as an image of the Western Paradise of the Pure Land at the very moment the souls of the blessed are received into its safekeeping.

This Jōdo-dō is notable as having survived structurally intact until disassembled for repairs in 1957. Shinohara's visit there took place either in late 1957, or sometime during 1958. This stark contrast between the distinctive but relatively unsophisticated exter-

nal appearance of the building with its square plan and vast pyramidal roof, all based on simple straight lines, and the overwhelming complexity and boldness of the hall's interior, fired the heart of the young and sensitive Shinohara.

THE REALM OF
INFLUENCE

In view of Shinohara's hope of restoring a place for the human spirit that he feared was disappearing from the living space of the modern age, it is unsurprising that he was drawn to these simple and clear geometrics, having become over time one defining aspect of Japanese tradition.

It was in House in Komae (1960) that Kazuo Shinohara first introduced the iconic pairing of a square plan and pyramidal roof to his own residential design. This sudden adaptation of a bold form and shape for House in Komae corresponds to the months just after Shinohara's visit to Jōdo-dō.

It is sometimes pointed out that the architect Gyōji Banshoya, a classmate of Shinohara's at Tokyo Tech, had earlier completed and published (*Shinkenchiku*, May 1953) a small house with a pyramidal roof. Yet Banshoya's house exemplifies neither the unique structural dimensioning nor any spatial tendency toward verticality, both qualities directly derived from Shinohara's experience at Jōdo-dō.

In East Asian Buddhism, the choice of a high-pitched hipped roof often covered in a sea of tiles and sometimes with the implied verticality of a pyramid, has long distinguished places of worship from ordinary living space, in much the same manner as the dome in West-

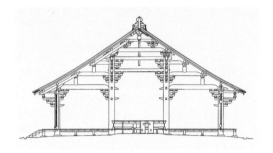

Jōdo-dō, Jōdo-ji, Ono,
Hyogo Prefecture, 1194, section

ern or Islamic architecture. Since their introduction into Japan together with Buddhism itself at the beginning of the sixth century (the so-called Asuka period, 550–710 CE), such pyramidal roofs gradually infiltrated Japanese tradition. Like the dome, the pyramidal form signals a purely spiritual outlook surpassing the tenets of any one religion.

THE DOMAIN OF STRUCTURE

House in Komae pursues an analogous arrangement of beams as at Jōdo-dō, albeit in a far less complex way. Its structural system supports a pyramidal roof via a composition of beams that materializes the crossed diagonals of the square plan. But its structure is concealed by a shallower, false pyramidal ceiling set just beneath these. Thus, the desired pyramidal shape was duly achieved by Shinohara both inside and out in the second-floor main space under the roof—but with all supporting members concealed from the viewer.

At Umbrella House (1961), the architect devised fan-rafters as a way of obviating the need for the diagonal tie-beams required at Komae; these fan-rafters span downward from the apex of the pyramidal roof and are intentionally exposed in the interior. The same kind of fan-rafter is used at Jōdo-dō, though it is visible only from each of the four corners. Thus, the visual expressiveness of the roof at Umbrella House amounts to a further development of its classical counterpart at Jōdo-dō, as it renders visible the whole of the exposed under-roof surface.

Nonetheless, the shape of Shinohara's umbrella-like roof is distinct from the overall spatial expression of the Jōdo-dō interior, with its four independent central pillars and plethora of horizontal structural elements, which from some positions are perceived as if flying through space. It would have been unreasonable to imagine squeezing the complex structural system at Ono into a miniscule house design. In addition to its fan-rafters, various other modifications characterize the Umbrella House structural system. To arrest the outward thrust that a pyramidal roof exerts, two major beams were orthogonally set on lines unequally bisecting the square plan four-to-three, thus constituting an east-west and a north-south axis. The smaller of the two spaces resulting from this dual bisection permits the installation of a lowered ceiling for a slightly raised tatami-room, while the other beam is left apparent in the floored main space and used to hang a wide bamboo screen (*sudare*) that serves to separate living and dining-kitchen spaces. However perfectly this composition corresponded with its overall structural solution in Shinohara's own mind, the vision of the unforgettable totality of the structural expression at Jōdo-dō must still have presented itself to him like a shimmering mirage.

Kazuo Shinohara, Umbrella House,
Nerima Ward, Tokyo, 1961, before occupation

"DECORATIVE SPACE"

Another early article by Shinohara, "The Three Primary Spaces" (*Shinkenchiku*, April 1964; English: *Japan Architect*, August 1964), is brief but key to understanding the DNA embodied in his First Style. He sets forth the qualifier "primary" in the sense inherent to "primary colors," namely as the three items from which all others derive. Accordingly, all archetypal built spaces blend Symbolic Space, Decorative Space, and Functional Space in various combinations. While this theorem-like presentation exemplifies Shinohara's personal character and methodology, his work of these years tends to a preoccupation with Decorative Space. The previous year, the architect had duly published a public "Memorandum on Decorative Space" in *Shinkenchiku* (November 1963). The following passage from *Jūtaku-kenchiku* (1964), already cited as his first book-length text and quoted above, provides a guarded confirmation of the preeminence of so-called Decorative Space.

I wish to clarify the fact that a tendency toward Decorative Space scarcely constitutes the whole of my current pursuit of space but is only a single aspect of it. As such, it is obvious that Decorative Space is indeed one of the major objectives I have sought throughout the series of my latest works.

Jūtaku-kenchiku, pp.163–164 [trans.]

Given Shinohara's way of thinking at this time, some notion would have been swirling within his head as to the way in which decoration, widely condemned by the Japanese architectural mainstream after World War II, must figure strongly at the cutting-edge, not just as mere superficial ornamentation on the façade of a building. This unusual approach is straightforwardly embodied in Shinohara's idea of rehabilitating the value of the house for the modern age by endowing residential architecture with spaces of what he refers to as colorful and glittering splendor. Such had historically been encountered only in the residences of elected officials, the Meiji-era aristocracy, or high-ranking military officials intended to function as an architecturally applied shorthand decorum.

Thus, at a single stroke, Shinohara also sweeps away belief in a naïvely held but by now derivative faith in the medieval aesthetic known as *"wabi-sabi,"* namely an acceptance of beauty perceived as "imperfect, impermanent, and incomplete," as originally articulated in the sixteenth century as the Buddhist-inspired core concept of Japanese beauty.

> It was [the German] Bruno Taut, one of the heroes of expressionist architecture, who called out the shogunal Tōshō-gū shrine [and mausoleum, at Nikko] as "Fake" or "Imitation," claiming it to be the "Ultimate Decadence in Architecture."
>
> Considered more deeply, [Taut's] evaluation of the shrine complex as "decadent" is not just a matter of art but also one of ethics.
>
> There is yet another cautionary aspect of reassessing Nikko Tōshō-gū, apart from Bruno Taut's "Decadence Hypothesis." It is the assertion of the shrine as being a "beautiful craftwork," a notion now widely supported. As a mere token of conventional wisdom, this presents little or no problem. But when architects are encouraged to view such huge structures as "craftwork" a suspension of judgment enters the equation.
>
> *Jūtaku-kenchiku*, pp. 165–166 [trans.]

In House in Chigasaki (1960), a bamboo blind interwoven with a thick, dyed-black cotton thread was hung to separate the main living space and dining room, with the assistance of a noted textile designer, a gesture that reoccurs more simply at Umbrella House. For the first time, Umbrella House features a suite of five small paintings, each of a size around

30 cm² square and themed on the motif of ancient sword guards, executed in rust vermilion with Japanese black ink on gold leaf paper. These were fixed on sliding partitions between the main room and the tatami-room, a contribution by the already celebrated painter and set-designer Setsu Asakura.

At House with a Big Roof (1961) and House with an Earthen Floor (1963), the whole of each was covered by a mono-roof with camber *(mukuri)*. In the case of House with a Big Roof, comparable in size to a stately residence of former days in Japan, the roof might well be regarded as an expression of the client's membership among the wealthier classes.

Kazuo Shinohara, House with a Big Roof, Ōta Ward, Tokyo, 1961

However, since the very same roof shape was conferred by Shinohara upon a small, simple mountain hut such as House with an Earthen Floor, this roof shape can hardly be related to mere social standing.

In fact, the cambered form with its *mukuri* is a symbolic expression used in the Japanese *sukiya* style, which governs the overall taste and architecture of the teahouse. It provides a sharp contrast with the formal convex curvature *(sori)* characteristic of Buddhist temple structures, including Jōdoji. So even though Shinohara's Decorative Space had been largely restricted to interiors until Umbrella House, concentration on roof shape largely unconnected to any functional aspect

North House in Hanayama, Kobe,
Hyogo Prefecture, 1965, main room

South House in Hanayama, Kobe,
Hyogo Prefecture, 1968, fissure space

may now be understood as pertaining to the trope of Decorative Space. Yet, the cambered shape is never again seen in any of Shinohara's works.

Thus, examining the series of Shinohara's early works and writings prior to and succeeding Umbrella House, we understand how among the three so-called primary spaces (Symbolic, Decorative and Functional), Shinohara had devoted significant attention to Decorative Space. Notably in Umbrella House itself, other than the fan-rafters that gave rise to its name and the artistic collaboration in the series of small vignettes by Setsu Asakura, there remains one further manifestation of Decorative Space consisting in the architect's delicate articulation of the ends of the projecting sub-beams at the front of the half-open attic.

What we have then is a very small house, embellished but sparingly so, that eschews any concept of "Decorative Space" as an old-fashioned manifestation of social decorum and personal status.

RHETORIC OF
THE PYRAMIDAL ROOF

After experimenting with several differently conceived intervening works, Shinohara reverted to a square plan with a pyramidal roof at Hanayama, a residential area overlooking Kobe. A North House (1965) and a South House (1968) designed for brothers stand chronologically on either side of the date of completion of the landmark House in White (1966) in Tokyo. However, we can suppose that the joint project for the two houses at Hanayama must have proceeded more or less in tandem.

> Compared with the three-quarter volume of an 11-meter square pyramidal shape of the North House, the slightly larger if similar form of the South House is reversed by an east-west layout and joined on site with the North House. [My] original intention was thus largely realized in built form with only slight modifications.
>
> "Interpretation of North House in Hanayama," *Shinkenchiku*, January 1969, p. 134 [trans.]

The tangentially joined houses at Hanayama, which are similar in external appearance but opposed in orientation—each based on the excision of a full quarter of its square-based

North House, 1965, and South House, 1968
in Hanayama, Kobe, Hyogo Prefecture, aerial view

North House, 1965 (above), and South House in
Hanayama (below), 1968, Kobe, Hyogo Prefecture,
first floor plans

pyramidal volume—are known for their significant divergence in interior treatment. North House, with its front-to-rear defined corridor, drawn from the reminiscence of a so-called *tōriniwa*, or narrow landscaped semi-outdoor passageway, belonged to one type of traditional Japanese town house. Meanwhile, South House in Hanayama, with its distinctively high-ceilinged void and narrow hall leading from the entrance to the main room, is one of several pioneering works that looks forward to the "Fissure Space" of Shinohara's later Second Style. Shinohara's handling of these differences is uniquely skilled in the evolving relationship between a pyramidal roof and its structural system, as this differs between the two houses.

In both houses at Hanayama, a central pillar supporting the apex of the pyramidal roof was required because the span was broader than at either House in Komae or Umbrella House (to be accurate, a composite pillar consisting of three substantial colonettes is used in South House). Meanwhile, considering the load of weighty Japanese tiles covering the roofs of both houses, an original system of diagonal struts was devised to yield support at the approximate midpoint of each main rafter that spans from the peak of the roof to the three equidistant corners of each plan. Though the central pillar of each Hanayama house is embedded within their common notched (i.e., L-shaped) floor plans,

the respective three struts radiate dramatically into the upper triangular void of both houses' main rooms with an overwhelming presence. It thereby seems almost as if a return to the amazing internal structural expression at Jōdo-dō, which had been impossible to express directly in Umbrella House, were being attempted at Hanayama.

Having only just completed the design of North House in Hanayama, Shinohara finalized his design for House in White the following year. Even today, House in White enjoys the highest reputation of all his many residential works. Its 10-meter square plan, surmounted by a perfect pyramidal roof, comes closest to Jōdo-dō of any of his works.

The structural system supporting this pyramidal roof by a central column of burnished Higashiyama cedar and four concealed diagonal struts spreading from somewhat above its midpoint is clearly a development from the structure of North House in Hanayama. But at House in White this straightforward structural application is nonetheless hidden, as it was at Komae, by the imposition of a false ceiling. Thus, the central column is only partially revealed within the pure, white, cuboid main living room. Moreover, as the floor plan is unequally bisected by a two-story non-bearing wall placed one meter or so behind the central column, this pillar, while centered vis-à-vis the overall structural system, appears eccentrically placed within the main room. In this way, the view of this central column against the background of the internal wall plays a principal role in imposing the "spatial frontality" that features in virtually all traditional Japanese architecture and was still clung to by Shinohara in his First Style: the pillar's undue slenderness seems to deny the perception of perspective depth. All this succeeds in creating a barrier between the unseen efficiency of structural forces and the phenomenal aspect of spatial experience on the part of the observer. Shinohara noted at the time:

> I have attempted a square plan several times till now. Among these, [House in White] is the largest, but I have tried nonetheless to simplify its spatial composition.

> My concern with the style of Japanese architecture began with my first work. Another methodological focus—the potential of an abstract space—has continually persisted alongside [any notion of style]. This pairing occurred from the outset, as abstract space is in no way divorced from the style of Japanese traditional space; so for me, both factors easily coexisted. But, in the most basic terms, the underlying preoccupation with abstract space began to strengthen, and in my mind the balance between these two interests is still shifting.

> To form an abstract space by peeling away little by little its Japanese appearance, I am inclined to refocus on our daily lives, but this is no easy achievement. While the search for abstrac-

tion rooted in an ever more perfected form accompanies this exercise, yet a still different phase of spatial reality is now already occupying my mind.

"Interpretation of House in White,"
Shinkenchiku, July 1967, p. 124 [trans.]

House in White, long recognized as the masterpiece of the First Style, not least by Shinohara's own stipulation, is also a heroic attempt to revive the abstract essence of Japanese traditional space in the modern age. From the

Kazuo Shinohara, House in White,
Suginami Ward, Tokyo, 1966, main room,
section and first floor plan

moment of its completion, the house denoted a newborn sense of freedom from Japanese tradition, as a fulfillment of the next "phase" already "occupying [his] mind." Within five or less years we shall see the primacy of a white compressed cuboid principal room but without the least connection to Shinohara's neo-traditional pyramidal roof belonging to the earlier suite of houses.

So, starting out in Komae, followed by Umbrella House as a turning point, the joint evolution of North and South Houses in Hanayama, and House in White—all Shinohara's design activity of this mid-sixties period had centered upon unifying a square plan and pyramidal roof. He oscillated between his devotion to Jōdo-dō and an anticipated liberation from that very same emblem of millennial tradition—all the while half-suppressing, half-anticipating a *next* space, that of the Second Style.

MATHEMATICAL SPACE AND "A HOUSE IS ART"

Mathematics is thought of as a world of abstract beauty situated at the point furthest from architecture, which in contrast is favored with an extreme physical embodiment. For Shinohara this was idiomatic, given his own mathematical studies prior to concentrating on architecture at Tokyo Tech. In

Kazuo Shinohara, House in Komae, Tokyo, 1960, section and second floor plan

Umbrella House he strove to attain a coexistence between the vernacular *minka* residence, a form without formal logic yet supported by long custom, and his own universal mathematical world view. Possibly, some notion was bedeviling Shinohara that he must unearth an ideal prototype behind the various typologies of *minka* in terms of a unique underlying mathematical beauty. If so, he would have wished to de-emphasize any mere accident of human habitation and work toward adapting the notion of the "commoner's dwelling" to the new rhythms of human life in a postwar modernist age.

It was because of Kazuo Shinohara's dual background in mathematics and architecture that he was able to extract an exciting idea regarding the modern dwelling that leaps out in his celebrated aphorism "A House Is Art." Though this battle cry was surely meant to stress the concept of his own kind of beauty rooted in mathematics, any exactitude proved elusive.

Among the earliest of his works, Umbrella House tends strongly to assert beauty as linked to constructional phenomena. As Shinohara later explained in his *Complete Works*:

> There remained [unimposing] vegetable fields in the surroundings of Umbrella House, the smallest house I've ever designed. Owing to lack of any transport from the railway station to the site, I sometimes had to walk for about 40 minutes there and back in cold winter weather. During one of those treks, it suddenly dawned that it is only when a house becomes a work of art that the significance of an architect concentrating all his effort into a small private building is justified. It was at the time of Umbrella House's original publication that my [aphorism] "A House Is Art" formulated itself. Failing actual experience of those golden days of functionalism, rationalism, and technocracy, the significance and risk of such a declaration is [today] scarcely appreciable.
>
> *Kazuo Shinohara Complete Works,*
> TOTO Shuppan, 1996, p. 63

This axiom, abounding in confidence and an ability to self-adapt, later came to be accepted as emblematic of Shinohara's character. But from the above remarks pronounced later in life we know that the idea was only grasped via a gradually maturing awareness on the architect's part. A *koan*-like admission suddenly crossing the mind of a largely inexperienced young architect working in complete isolation and trudging to the building site with a raging, ice-cold wind at his back.

What is meant is that house design be-
comes independent of the more general
field of architecture. Its identity as
"housing" shifts to the more
individualized domain shared with
the arts of painting, sculpture, or liter-
ature, and the rest.

"A House Is Art," *Shinkenchiku*, May 1962,
p. 77 [trans.]

At that time, two years before the Tokyo
Olympics in 1964, erection of all kinds of
buildings and a vastly extended infrastruc-
ture was proceeding with unprecedented
haste. In such conditions, architecture was
scarcely regarded as an artistic domain, having become synonymous with Japan's rena-
scent building industry. With scarcely a side-
long glance at this new embodiment of Tokyo,
with jack hammer ringing day and night, Shinohara challenged the mainstream with his
untoward aphorism: "A House Is Art." Not
surprisingly, this was widely misunderstood
as a measure of justification for his own am-
bitions while neglecting the client's needs.

Faced with the earlier experience of Umbrella House, he asked himself whether the "Art"
embodied in a house could best be devel-
oped via "Decoration" or "Abstraction." That
dilemma is most explicit in his description of
House in White quoted above.

In a 1997 interview, Shinohara declared to a
younger critic Terunobu Fujimori the gist of
his intention at Umbrella House: "Behind its
composition, this house is rooted in mathematics [...]." His response followed years of
practice that had erased any doubt the architect might once have felt. Would he have
replied so decisively thirty years earlier
when Umbrella House had only just been
completed, a time when he had worked so
stubbornly to achieve a "Decorative Space"
both here and in the several houses that followed? Umbrella House is also the first work
explicitly declared as seeking to align Shinohara's First Style with Japanese tradition as

its main theme, so can we say that the turning point from "Decoration" to "Abstraction"
is securely located here?

The five years from 1961 to 1966 when Shinohara's thought oscillated between Umbrella
House and House in White, have been inter-
preted as a period of soul-searching. The
resulting turning point from decoration to
abstraction was inevitably bound up with
the future of his theory and methods, and it
impacted the architect's entire career from
the mid-1960s onward.

DNA, UMBRELLA
HOUSE, AND A RETURN
TO JŌDO-DŌ

In the late 1950s, Shinohara's determination
to integrate Chōgen's unusual square floor
plan with its pyramidal roof into his own
work began with his game-changing encoun-
ter at Jōdo-dō. Via House in Komae and more
unmistakably at Umbrella House, this rhe-
torical development might be assumed to
terminate with House in White. However,
the latter's interior space wholly diverged
from that of Jōdo-dō, as explained above.
The Pure Land Hall obviously displays neither the bisected floor plan that became an
important hallmark of Shinohara's First Style
nor the sectional partition that allows for either full or partial concealment of the roof
structure. Meanwhile, the white cuboid interior at House in White, where the half-ex-
posed cedar pillar supporting the roof is perceived to "float," draws a thorough contra-
distinction with the assimilated simplicity of
the "Great Buddha Style" exterior of the
dwelling itself. House in White indeed rep-
resents the most celebrated articulation of
the First Style, while the pronounced verticality of the main room connects it with the
Second Style, which was about to emerge unexpectedly by way of the treatment of this
very space, an event that even Shinohara himself fully perceived only with the gradual
passage of time.

Afterward, his oeuvre traversed a brief Second Style comprising some ten works designed on variants of a so-called Fissure Space, which grew from the cuboid interior that House in White had unwittingly brought into being. From the mid-1970s, Shinohara turned (once again gradually and himself only half aware of the transition) to what would emerge as his more varied Third Style, proposing various analogical alternatives to the ever-mutating chaos of the expanding Tokyo metropolis.

Finally, after witnessing (almost in the role of a spectator) a two-phase revolution in his own style, Kazuo Shinohara's passion for Jōdo-dō, which had so moved him as a young man, seemed to vanish. Since he had declared with authority at the beginning of the 1960s that "Tradition can only be a

Kazuo Shinohara, House on a Curved Road,
Shibuya Ward, Tokyo, 1978

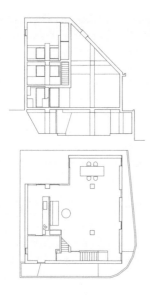

Kazuo Shinohara, House on a Curved Road,
Shibuya Ward, Tokyo, 1978, section and first
floor plan

starting point, never a point of return," even at a time when he was himself excitedly engaging with Japanese tradition, it seems almost a reversal of logic that the spatial module he himself had put forward was itself

liable to transition. Still, his affection for Jōdo-dō persisted subconsciously, the burning of a slight but constant flame.

Taking a precise example, neither the plan of House on a Curved Road (1978) is an absolute square nor is the roof symmetrical; yet, when we examine its plan, elevation, and section together, it is nonetheless apparent that the outer envelope combines a little over a 10 m² floor plan and a near pyramidal roof inclined at 45 degrees. Nor can we deny that its four soaring independent pillars each of a 450 mm² square profile, set at the plan's center at intervals of 4.5 m, are reminiscent of the innermost configuration at Jōdo-dō. Likewise, uniformly dimensioned beams penetrate these pillars to produce an elevated three-dimensional grid that extends to the outer walls and roof. These interlocking verticals and horizontals furnish the house's core structure yet are only visible in part.

About half of this system—which if fully exposed would be viewed as a consistent space frame—is interwoven with a series of small upper rooms. Nevertheless, enough of the overall three-dimensional concrete framing is visible from the large first-floor main room as it soars dramatically upward through four stories for us to envision the integrity of the full gridded form. All this makes for a combined abstraction and austerity—frequently referred to as being distinctly "Shinohara-esque." Yet it must also be seen as a re-adaptation of the Jōdo-dō interior as the young architect had bodily experienced it.

In a later dialog with noted fellow architect Arata Isozaki, Shinohara sought to convey his mental attitude toward this dramatically site-constrained house:

> When I had completed House on a Curved Road, one thread of public criticism had it that "symbolic shadows were once again reemerging." In this house I believed that I had produced a very dry exercise, but in fact a certain spiritual aspect linked to my previous work was slipping back in as remnant of [my] past, a fact I could not deny.
>
> [The frame of House on a Curved Road was] a purely morphological datum in the shape of a gridded outline—just as what I had tried to make it. Yet, once the pyramidal roof overhead had been put in place, I felt as if a modicum of meaning were still being eked out.
>
> Owing to the unusual and imposing ceiling height in the main living space, it would have been impossible to avoid all degree of expressiveness. Yet since the choice of such a high ceiling carries its own symbolic charge, it was no surprise that [the proverbial armchair critic] could easily find here a reappearance of the symbolism [inherent to my earlier work].
>
> "About Modernism," *Shinkenchiku*,
> January 1981, pp. 192–193 [trans.]

As stated, by the latter half of the 1970s Shinohara was searching outside the Functional, Decorative, and Symbolic spaces, three domains all rooted in Japanese tradition. He began to seek out an Abstract Space: this time one without the least associated, or "symbolic," meanings, even though it too is a realm easily discernible in Japanese tradition. Amid Shinohara's at first largely theoretical research, the motions of his own hand in designing actual spaces began to recall to him his early, more physical and emotive experiences at Jōdo-dō.

For it is little known that in the latter part of his career, Shinohara created countless multi-colored concept sketches in colored pencil, in an attempt to advance his architectural work as a continuum of "styles." The dialog with Arata Isozaki emphasizes a deep somatic impetus on Shinohara's part. It also confirms how Shinohara had long adhered to a strict temporal development, re-examining episodes of his own style to achieve his next goals. Still, it may be hard for a younger generation necessarily more familiar with Shinohara's more publicly accessible Fourth Style works to comprehend how his several changes of "style" were consistently backed by his interrogation of Japanese tradition.

If Umbrella House marks a nascent split in the early 1960s from his so-called Decorative Space to his at the time recently conceived Abstract Space, his House on a Curved Road a decade and a half later signifies a reconfluence of the two streams. Accordingly, House on a Curved Road should be read as a direct reinterpretation of Jōdo-dō, which had so deeply moved Shinohara in his youth; no longer via the route of Decorative Space or Symbolic Space, but instead grasping what he had now begun to refer to as Abstract Space. Those works of Shinohara's that follow House on a Curved Road belong to a generally more unified stage of the architect's activity. As the subtitle for the introductory paragraph of the Isozaki dialog has it, he was altogether "breaking away from a space of meaning."

After House on a Curved Road, designs of a building with only a single unified roof form disappear altogether from Shinohara's practice. The concept of a "big roof" is said

Kondō of Tōshōdai-ji, Nara, Nara Prefecture,
710–794

to date from Shinohara's very early visit in the late 1940s to the kondō or Golden Hall of the eighth-century Tōshōdai-ji in the outskirts of Nara, before he had begun to study architecture. Tōshōdai-ji is believed to have provided him with inspiration to change from a further study of mathematics to the pursuit of architecture. The Golden Hall, with its vast single story, hipped tiled roof surmounting a seven-bay façade, is considered an archetypical example of the classical Tang-dynasty Chinese Buddhist style as imported to Japan. Later, Shinohara declared in an essay introducing his own so-called House with a Big Roof:

> The overwhelming impact [i.e., his first visit to Tōshōdai-ji], with its prominent roofing tiles shimmering like a silver curtain in a mist of dissipating rain, may have returned via my design for this house even after fifteen years have passed. I have at last been able to find an appropriate situation for realizing the desire that lay dormant for such a long time to revive this kind of extraordinary big roof in our own time.
> Jūtaku-kenchiku, 1964, p. 159 [trans.]

Starting from Umbrella House and after grounding several more works in the notion of Decorative Space, Shinohara was preparing the way toward an Abstract Space. Yet, albeit theoretically discarded, Decorative

Space continued to breathe life into his later works in different ways. In concrete terms Decorative Space was to enjoy a long life in the combination of extreme Japanese-style colors such as employed in House on a Curved Road or in erotic or ornamental furniture designs, made as showpieces notably for House in Yokohama (1985). In this way, Decorative Space plays a back-up role in perpetuating individual somatic desire in the series of otherwise at times stoically Abstract Spaces that occur in works of both his Third and Fourth Styles.

Many aspects of Shinohara's essential activities, such as the combination of diverse structural systems with heterogenous spatial compositions, a diversifying overlap of Decorative with Abstract Spaces, as well as geometrical with more conjectural mathematical thinking, already characterize Umbrella House. As recalled by the celebrated aphorism "A House is Art," we may well regard this as integral to the chain of genes and their expression such as characterize each of Shinohara's succeeding works, and that in spite of the quite modest dimensions of Umbrella House as we now see it reconstructed here at Vitra.

BIOGRAPHY
KAZUO SHINOHARA (1925–2006)

From a 21ˢᵗ-century perspective, Kazuo Shinohara, who initially trained as a mathematician, has arguably become the most significant Japanese architect active in the postwar period aside from Kenzo Tange (1913–2005). Soon after graduating from Tokyo Institute of Technology in 1953, he started his own one-man design practice while serving as an Assistant at Tokyo Institute of Technology. Ten years later he was named Associate Professor and in 1964 published his first book *Residential Architecture* [*Jūtaku-kenchiku*, English-language version forthcoming], Tokyo. This was followed by numerous writings and books, as well as published discourses and interviews.

In 1967 he received his Doctor of Engineering at Tokyo Institute of Technology and was promoted to the rank of Full Professor. Shinohara's built work, which consists largely of single-family houses, is divided into a series of self-designated "Four Styles."

Umbrella House (1961), to which this book is dedicated, is one of the principal works of his First Style (1954–69). His Second Style (1970–74) of ten ostensibly Modernist residences, largely of reinforced concrete, ended with the minimalist Prism House (1974). In 1972 Shinohara traveled for the first time abroad, visiting North Africa and Europe. This trip was intriguingly followed in 1975 by a brief solo trip to West Africa. Back in Japan, he realized a masterpiece of his Third Style (1974–82), House in Uehara (1976), a monolithic concrete dwelling surmounted during the construction phase by a semi-cylindrical steel vaulted room. House in Yokohama (1984) marked the beginning of the even more disjunctive Fourth Style (1984–). Kazuo Shinohara was the recipient of the First Golden Lion in Memoriam (2010), conferred at the 12ᵗʰ Architectural Biennale in Venice, in addition to a growing contingent of other awards and prizes throughout his life.

CONTRIBUTORS

CHRISTIAN DEHLI, ANDREA GROLIMUND
Architects trained at the Swiss Federal Institute of Technology, Zurich (ETHZ). After graduating, they established the architectural practice DEHLI GROLIMUND in Zurich, Switzerland (2019) and in the same year jointly published *Kazuo Shinohara: 3 Houses*, in addition to articles on numerous architectural topics. As co-architects, they supervised the reconstruction of Kazuo Shinohara's Umbrella House on the Vitra Campus in Weil am Rhein, Germany (2021–2022).

RYUE NISHIZAWA
Architect who co-founded the firm SANAA (1995) in Tokyo, Japan, together with Kazuyo Sejima. Two years later he established the Office of Ryue Nishizawa. Nishizawa was recently appointed Professor at the Yokohama Graduate School of Architecture, Yokohama National University. SAANA was awarded the Pritzker Prize in 2010.

SHIN-ICHI OKUYAMA
Architect trained at Tokyo Institute of Technology (Tokyo Tech), where he graduated from the lab of Kazunari Sakamoto. He maintains a small private practice and is a Professor at Tokyo Tech, where he teaches Architectural Design and Theory. An authority on the work of Kazuo Shinohara, he has published and edited various books and essays about the architect, whose work and livelihood he generously facilitated in the final years of the latter's career.

DAVID B. STEWART
Architectural historian who graduated from the University of Pennsylvania and the Courtauld Institute of Art, London University, earning a PhD under Sir Nikolaus Pevsner. He is a Professor Emeritus at Tokyo Institute of Technology (Tokyo Tech), where he was a friend and longtime colleague of Kazuo Shinohara.

BUILDING FACTS
UMBRELLA HOUSE

PROJECT
Location: Hayamiya, Nerima Ward, Tokyo,
Japan, relocated to Vitra Campus, Weil am Rhein,
Germany in 2022
Architect: Kazuo Shinohara
Structural engineer: Kazuhide Tsuge
Furniture design: Kazuo Shinohara,
Katsuhiko Shiraishi
Artworks: Setsu Asakura
Contractor: Watanabe Architectural Contractors
Structure: Timber
Furniture manufacturers: Soken-sha, Aoshima Sho-
ten, Tendo Mokko Furniture Co.

SITE AND FLOOR AREAS
Site area: 187.2 m²
Total floor area: 72.3 m²
First floor: 55.4 m²
Second floor: 16.9 m²

RECONSTRUCTION TEAM TOKYO TECH
Architectural direction: Prof. Shin-ichi Okuyama
Project architect: Research Associate Masaru Otsuka;
assisted by Koshiro Ogura and Yutaro Honshuku
Heritage consultant: Heritage Houses Trust
and Prof. David B. Stewart, Tokyo, Japan
Structural engineering consultant:
Yoshiharu Kanebako, Kanebako Structural Engineers
Surveying and conservation: Prof. Taisuke Yamazaki;
assisted by Naoto Kizu
Dismantling and repair: Hidemitsu Ogura and
Yusuke Fuchita, Fuhki Construction, Tokyo, Japan

RECONSTRUCTION TEAM VITRA
Reconstruction co-architects:
Christian Dehli, Andrea Grolimund,
DEHLI GROLIMUND, Zurich, Switzerland
Site project manager: Christian Germadnik,
Logad GmbH, Weil am Rhein, Germany

COMPANIES INVOLVED IN RECONSTRUCTION
Builder: Binder & Blum GmbH, Schopfheim, Germany
Carpenters: Fuhki Construction, Tokyo, Japan;
Zimmerei Vogt GmbH, Lörrach, Germany
Cabinet maker: Schreinerei Volker Bäuchle,
Weil am Rhein, Germany
Roofer: Rathberger GmbH, Efringen-Kirchen, Germany
Plumber: Wolfgang Armbruster GmbH,
Weil am Rhein, Germany
Painters: Die Malermeister Beckert GmbH, Lörrach,
Germany; assisted by Giulia Pessi Maleratelier
GmbH, Basel, Switzerland
Gardener: Eise, Weil am Rhein, Germany
Electrician: Vitra Services GmbH,
Weil am Rhein, Germany
Restoration fusuma: Hiratate Hyogu Maker,
Tokyo, Japan
Replica Shoji and window frames: Nishijima Tategu
Maker, Tokyo, Japan

INTERIOR FINISHES
Silk wallpaper: Erimo Industries Co. Ltd., Kyoto, Japan
Tatami: Morita tatami mat maker, Tokyo, Japan
Tiles: Tajimi Custom Tiles, Tajimi, Japan;
assisted by David Glättli, Zurich, Switzerland

CUSTOM FURNITURE
Replica furniture: Schreinerei Wolfgang
Fünfgeld, Müllheim, Germany; upholstered by Modo
GmbH, Weil am Rhein, Germany
Furniture restoration: Elke von Hirschhausen,
Zell im Wiesental, Germany
Dining chairs: Jasper Morrison, customized HAL Ply,
Vitra, Germany, 2012/22

LIGHTING
Replica ceiling lamp: Miura Shomei Co. Ltd.,
Kyoto, Japan
Pendent lamps: Mogens Koch, Le Klint 105
large paper, Le Klint, Denmark, 1945

ACCESSORIES
Bamboo screen: Suzumatsu Shoten Co. Ltd.,
Tokyo, Japan
Carpet: Oriental Carpet Mills Ltd., Yamagata, Japan
Ikebana: Suzue Rother-Nakaya, Gebenstorf, Switzer-
land; assisted by Chaoyu Du, Zurich, Switzerland

CHRONOLOGY

PROJECT
Design: 1959/12 – 1960/09
Construction: 1960/11 – 1961/03
Completion: 1961/03
Furniture: 1961/03 – 1962/09
First published in *Shinkenchiku*: 1962/10

SURVEY AND RESTORATION
Survey: 2020/03 – 2020/09
Dismantling: 2020/06 – 2020/08
Design for relocation: 2020/09 – 2021/12
Restoration of wooden structure:
2020/09 – 2021/03
Shipping: 2021/05 – 2021/06

RECONSTRUCTION
Container arrival: 2021/06
Reconstruction: 2021/07 – 2022/07
Completion: 2021/07
Inauguration: 2022/11

ACKNOWLEDGMENTS

First, we wish to thank Rolf Fehlbaum of Vitra for volunteering to preserve Kazuo Shinohara's Umbrella House for future generations, as well as for making this publication possible. We also thank the Vitra Design Museum, especially Esther Schröter, for her abiding trust and efficient collaboration. Furthermore, we would like to acknowledge Naoko Hirai and Eri Ashihara from Vitra Japan for their efforts and patience in helping us secure various copyrights.

It is impossible not to mention the support of Tokyo Tech, namely Professors Shin-ichi Okuyama and David B. Stewart, who always stood by with their personal firsthand knowledge of the architect, while contributing an informative text concerning the genealogy of the house. We also wish to thank Masaru Otsuka and Koshiro Ogura at Tokyo Tech for their assistance in resolving technical considerations.

Very special thanks go to Ryue Nishizawa for sharing his perception of Umbrella House through his article. Emi Kawai has been invaluable in sharing historical family photos with the general public, as well as firsthand memories of the house.

We must not forget all those involved in production of the book itself: members of the graphic design studio Elektrosmog, namely Marco Walser, Natalie Rickert, and Marina Brugger, who have created a fine book through countless discussions and a lively mail correspondence. Finally, many thanks to the architectural photographer Damian Poffet, who shot a splendid recent series of photographs of Umbrella House, inside and out, largely included herein.

A big thank you goes to our families and friends who supported us, and especially to our two young sons Henrik and Niels for their patience when at times the book seemed to come first.

CREDITS

PHOTOS

pp. 1–8, pp. 113–120: Damian Poffet
pp. 19–30: Shozo Kawai © Emi Kawai
pp. 33–48, pp. 100–101, p. 103: Osamu Murai
pp. 58–59 (left), pp. 62–63, p. 65 (left), p. 67:
Sadamu Saito
p. 59 (right), p. 61, p. 64, p. 65 (right):
Tokyo Tech/ Taisuke Yamazaki Lab
p. 60: Heritage Houses Trust
p. 66, pp. 68–69: Tokyo Tech/
Shin-ichi Okuyama Lab
pp. 70–72: Megumi Ishikawa © Vitra Japan
pp. 80–94: DEHLI GROLIMUND
p. 97: Chuji Hirayama
p. 99: Yoshikazu Harada
p. 102: Koji Taki © Kazuo Shinohara Estate
p. 106: Shinkenchiku-sha
p. 108: Arthur Drexler

PLANS

Cover, pp. 52–55: DEHLI GROLIMUND
All Umbrella House plans are redrawn by the editors
from the original working drawings and verified
against the originals on behalf of the Kazuo Shinohara Estate.
p. 98: *Renovation Report of National Treasure Jōdo-ji
Jōdo-dō*, Renovation Committee of National Treasure
Jōdo-ji Jōdo-dō, 1959
pp. 102–104, p. 106: Tokyo Tech/ Kazuo Shinohara
Lab © Kazuo Shinohara Estate

TEXT

p. 31: Kazuo Shinohara, *Kazuo Shinohara: 16 Houses
and Architectural Theory*, Bijutsu Shuppan-sha,
Tokyo, 1971. Translation by Ikumi Hoshino emended.

COLOPHON

KAZUO SHINOHARA
THE UMBRELLA HOUSE PROJECT

Editors: Christian Dehli, Andrea Grolimund
Translation: Alan Gleason, Tokyo
Line editor: David B. Stewart
Copy editing and proofreading:
Benjamin Liebelt, Berlin
Graphic design: Elektrosmog, Zurich
Marina Brugger, Natalie Rickert, Marco Walser
Pre-press, printing and binding: DZA Druckerei
zu Altenburg GmbH, Altenburg, Germany
Distribution: Pinar Yildiz, Vitra Design Museum,
Weil am Rhein
Image use and supervison: Christian Dehli,
Andrea Grolimund
Paper: Inapa Bavaria Gloss, Munken Print White
Typefaces: Kozuka Mincho Pro

Vitra Design Museum
Charles-Eames-Str. 2
79576 Weil am Rhein
Germany
verlag@design-museum.de
www.design-museum.de

First edition
ISBN 978-3-945852-55-2
Printed and bound in Germany